Daniel
The Miracle Beagle

Joe Dwyer

First published by Dog Ear Publishing
4010 W. 86th Street, Ste H
Indianapolis, IN 46268
www.dogearpublishing.net

ISBN: 978-1-4575-1230-8

This book is printed on acid-free paper.

Printed in the United States of America

Scientists estimate that there are
700 billion animals in the world.

TABLE OF CONTENTS

There are 500 million dogs in the world.

INTRODUCTION

DOUGLAS LEVISON

CEO / CREATIVES

FLOWER POWER CREATIVE

Introduction

CEO/Creatives - Flower Power Creative

Daniel's Miracle arises from the highest, most dynamic, Qualities Of Life - Love, Peace, Compassion, Courage, Family and Community.

The power of a single life can touch - and change - the world. Daniel's winning charm and vivacity as he comes to resonate with so many people are living proof.

Daniel trotted away from an inconceivable ordeal - completely vibrant and free - to make his way into the hearts and minds of people throughout the world.

The network of people and organisations who - individually and collectively - first saved Daniel, and then carried on to deliver him to a warm and loving Forever Family, is proof that the infinite will to initiate positive, permanent change leads to astonishing accomplishments and great, shared joy.

Joe Dwyer - with the fullest support and dedication of his loving family and universe of friends - has worked, hand in paw, with Daniel on a mission to spread the word on a vital issue - the rescue, and adoption by Forever Families, of millions of magnificent Animal Companions around the world.

Joe's devotion - to people and animals - runs through the patterns of his life. His years of work as a Certified Dog Trainer / Animal Rescue Advocate - and in Civic and Corporate Mediation - expresses the totality of his caring.

Joe's background - and remarkable skills - as a Motivational Speaker, with the talents and ability to bring important points to life and so energize action for change across a broad front of essential social values and considerations, makes him the ideal spokesman for Daniel's Mission and the precious, most meaningful cause they champion.

Flower Power Creative is proud - and delighted - to collaborate with Daniel and Joe in structuring the most dynamic elements in all avenues of Media, Social Networks and Outreach to succeed in the rapid raising of Public Awareness around the planet as momentum grows toward accomplishing our mission.

As a Multi-Media / Multi-Platform – Politics / Music And Fine Arts / Women's Rights / Technology / Environment - Organisation, Flower Power Creative is fully committed to social progress and the development of solutions on a global scale.

We believe in the infinite ability of people to coalesce in creating a whole greater than the sum of the parts as they fulfill their vision across the broadest range of situations.

It is an honour - and a very great joy - to share Daniel's Miracle, his mission with Joe, and the story of a great victory of Life and Bliss, with the world.

Douglas Levison
CEO / CREATIVES - FLOWER POWER CREATIVE

There are 600 million cats in the world.

CHAPTER 1

DAY OF THE MIRACLE

THROUGH DANIEL'S EYES

Chapter One

Day of the Miracle
Through Daniel's Eyes

My Name is Daniel.

I'm a Beagle mix puppy, and this is where my miracle story begins.

Sharing all that I'm about to tell you is my way of giving thanks for every second of my life - everything that I've seen through, the dream come true of now, and the wonder of all happiness that is on the horizon.

Please join me as we share my journey.

I had started my life as a stray.

After a very short time roaming the streets, I was scooped up and taken into a so-called " Animal Control Center " in Alabama.

There are so many animals looking for a Forever Family - a home filled with love and peace for the rest of their lives.

There are millions of people - in all sorts of situations that arise in life - whose lives would be so much happier and richer in every way, with the love of a friendly and faithful pet.

Yet the reality - for far too long - is that the connection between pets and people, one that could be so easily arranged, is replaced by millions of us losing our lives - and millions of people and families losing out on our companionship - every year.

The rule at the "Center" where I'd been taken was that all dogs there were given four days to be adopted - or rescued toward being adopted. If - after the four days came and went - a dog was still there, that dog is finished in this world.

The Day Of Reckoning for me - and 18 other dogs - had arrived.

Words could never begin to describe the horror.

All of us were gathered together by two men. One seemed only to be interested in getting the "job" over with. The other couldn't even look me in the eye.

People speak in terms of "Doing unto others as you would have done unto you."

Some see that concept as philosophical or spiritual - others as religious. Such a simple, universal rule of excellent faith - it has guided good people for thousands of years.

In either case, what was being done to us was infinitely wrong. We were - all 19 of us - innocent creatures. We deserved a much greater chance to make our way and find a home. We needed much more time. Where were people with hearts and minds to save us?

Now, accepting our fate seemed to be all that was left.

We were herded together and then led down a long corridor.

There were some acts of resistance from some of the other dogs - snarling and biting as they fought for their lives. All they tried to do to save themselves only came and went as the march carried on.

Most of the rest of the poor creatures there were petrified.

Suddenly, the walking stopped.

Next – roughly and swiftly – we were shoveled into a tiny, dark chamber. Everything went black. All the other dogs around me panicked, trembled, whimpered and sobbed. A foul-smelling gas filled the air and – within what seemed to be both a lifetime and not time – the other 18 dogs were gone.

Somehow - after seeing through 20 minutes of bedlam and carnage - I had survived an inconceivable ordeal.

I trotted out - completely intact in heart and soul, body and mind.

How and why had I survived?

One of the two men who had been responsible for the carnage of the day looked at me - marveling at my heartiness and good fortune. He smiled and said that I obviously was meant to live.

Nature had given me the most precious gift - a second chance to live.

As the story of my survival makes its way out into the world, many people are calling what happened a miracle - an event that the usual laws of logic or science can't explain, and an example of how fantastic life can be - for everyone.

I believe that I've been given a purpose - to serve as an inspiration for all of us who share Love as we work together toward a time - as soon as possible - that all animals who can be saved go on to make their lives - and the lives of the people who open their homes and hearts to them - beautiful, bright, and free.

There are 220 million domestic cats
in the world.

CHAPTER 2
THREADS OF DESTINY
JOE

Chapter Two

Threads of Destiny

Joe

"**P**lease return to your seats, turn off all electronics and fasten your seat belts. We're beginning our decent into DFW International Airport."

My mind was running through some ideas I had planned to incorporate into a speech I was drafting, but as the flight attendant's voice rang loud over the intercom I sat upright, obeyed the command to switch off all electronics and prepared for the Fort Worth, Texas landing.

I was scheduled to speak at a PLPA, Pet Loss Professional Association conference the following day. It was a warm Sunday afternoon, and a heavy veil of humidity hung low, enveloping me in a tepid, almost suffocating, mist.

I had been asked to open a two-day workshop of the Pet Loss Professional Association with a motivational speech. Plans for an appearance at a school in New Jersey on Tuesday made the time in Texas even more precious.

Though energized and excited, I was suddenly overpowered by an uncanny feeling - one of those indefinable sensations that left me intrigued by the intuitive flow. I could not discern the nature of the feeling. Instead, I accepted it as too subtle to interpret. Shrugging my shoulders, I cleared my head and prepared for the landing. Thankfully, it was smooth and uneventful.

Racing through the airport, I searched for the exit signs, crossed the threshold dividing air conditioning cool from Fort Worth heat and hailed a taxi. Within moments I was speeding to my destination. Relaxing for the first time in almost twenty-four hours felt rejuvenating. I began to feel pretty secure about my speech - centered on the dog's view of leadership. A well-researched topic, I often found it inspirational and to the point in a lighthearted way.

Behind the smiles, I knew my audience would be enlightened. It happened with steady repetition. Certainly, I was eager to share my thoughts at the workshop.

Dogs are my passion. I love to love them. I love to train them. I love to help them embrace their missions to assist and form relationships with mankind.

Through my volunteer work at several shelters in New Jersey my attention was drawn to the world of abandoned dogs. I try my best - together with other animal lovers who equally give time to search for solutions either through fostering or adoption. Consequently, before departing I had printed out several pictures of dogs that had been recently forsaken. Many were bound for a far too early end. I summoned the strength and determination to save them.

Was it possible that with over 78.2 million dogs living with families in the United States, there were others who faced such a cruel ending?

In a rush to catch my flight, I shoved the photos into my luggage with the intention to glance at them once I settled in the hotel. Ever since Fritz, a reddish-tan Dachshund with dwarfed, arched limbs, a bulging chest and an exaggeratedly elongated torso came into my life as a school boy, my passion for dogs was born.

An only child, I was sometimes moody and forlorn. Dear Fritz filled my life with joy and camaraderie, eventually earning status as the "little brother" I often wished for.

Throughout my growing-up years, my four-pawed companion was beside me. I not only realized the empowerment of his untiring loyalty and phenomenal devotion, but was propelled into a different mind-set as a result of the unending surplus of unconditional love he was always willing to offer me.

It was incredible. Fritz was always loyal, joining me as I played with toys and learned from books, and shared my parents' affections.

He was always happy and peaceful, kept our mischievous secrets, and was filled with love. We got along as all siblings should.

Who are you, Fritz? I often posed the question, eyeing him as he playfully wiggled his narrow hips and wagged his tail, trying to meet my gaze. His tiny head traveled from my toes to my face in a graceful upward sweep.

Why does Fritz have the ability and willingness to give so much while asking nothing in return? I asked this question over and over, wondering if there was a deep, complicated explanation I would understand once I reached adulthood. Perhaps the answer was - simply : That's how dogs were designed.

After all, we sometimes forget that Nature's Plan evolved with man and animal living in harmony - sharing not only the earth, but the love and respect vibrating in the heart of every living creature.

If I wanted to be prepared for the opening of the workshop, I realized that it was time to focus on the here and now. Reaching for the printouts of the dogs in need of a "life jacket", I sighed - questioning what could have possibly gone awry. My long experience with animals offered the confirmation that they honored their promises. The best people do the same.

As a rule of thumb, most people adore their pets, treating them as treasured family members.

Forever Families coddle and spoil their pets to the hilt with toys, accessories, salon visits and spa vacations. Utopia should be the gift for every dog. Many individuals need to learn much greater respect for their four-pawed friends – freeing them to live happier lives.

I offered a prayer of progress for all dogs looking for love, and then proceeded with my day. Someone had to give voice to these wonderful creatures, who only want to share love.

By now comfortably at the Embassy Suites Hotel in the heart of Sundance Square, I unpacked my belongings, then relaxed in an armchair to review my notes. Filed in the same folder were the photos of the abandoned shelter dogs. I'll admit it. I truly am a fanatical dog lover!

The first dossier held the photo of a beagle. His big wide-set eyes spoke of intelligence and an endearing playfulness. Such a soft-hearted little dog would surely compliment a family, especially one filled with the energy and laughter of children.

I had a big presentation in the morning. Developing answers to accelerating the pace of pet rescue and adoption could carry on to tomorrow.

I placed my presentation on the desk beside the photos of the dogs, walked into the bedroom, unwound from the day, and offered a prayer for the big-eyed beagle before drifting off to a deep sleep. There was something about his sweet face that tugged at my heartstrings.

The next morning was filled with sunlight. The day offered tremendous promise, as I got ready for my presentation.

I was feeling extremely upbeat. I phoned my wife, Geralynn, who reassured me that everyone and everything – home, family, four dogs - was fine.

My beautiful wife of twenty-five years had gotten approval from "little brother" Fritz. After sharing tales of school, sports, teen years and girls with him, I elicited Fritz's opinion before I asked Geralynn for her hand in marriage. Once her radiant smile met his glance, it was a done deal. He expressed his infinite love for her in a shower of kisses, and I proposed in a very short time.

Geralynn and I have two wonderful children - a son, Joe III, and a daughter, Jenna - both of whom are fervent animal lovers, like their parents.

The rest of the family is our canines:

Shelby – our rescued pit-bull - was set free from tremendous cruelty and suffering, fastened to a fence at a gas station. Surgery repaired her hind legs and a healthy diet gave her heart and strength. She has grown to be a beacon for compassionate therapy, adjusting to the loss of a pet, and eliminating bullying. Her mission touches the hearts of everyone she meets – inspiring and comforting as she continues her amazing journey. Sparty is our alpha dog. He, too, was given a brand new life with us. He loves the role of "big brother" to Rommel and Greta – two lovable Dachshunds who are great charmers, offering an abundance of total love to our family.

The photo of the Beagle pup flashed back to my awareness as I counted down to the presentation. His face filled me with the energy to find solutions for pets who deserved a new life.

All pups deserved a fair chance for adoption. Everyone – regardless of species – is born with a purpose. I wanted to do my part - everything I could – to defend their right to full and happy lives.

The power of this commitment could be channeled toward the more than 30 states where these precious friends needed protection for their right to live.

Within days, the cause that had started to stir within my awareness – with the Beagle pup at the heart of my desire to work for more and better – had merged with a sense of very great purpose. Far beyond my immediate situation, various threads were weaving together – soon to create a fantastic destiny.

There are 96 million pet cats
in the United States.

CHAPTER 3

STARTING POINT
THE RESCUE
DANIEL

Chapter Three

Starting Point—The Rescue
Daniel

"W hat's happening?" a strange voice asked. "Did I just hear a bark?"

From the corner of my eye, I saw a heavy-set man approach. I shut my eyes to save them from sand that came my way. Perhaps a bit of consideration for an abandoned dog was too much to ask. Actually pausing a moment to reflect, I guess it wasn't his fault. He was merely doing his sorry job I doubt he wanted to purposely add to my grief.

Humans have a funny way of walking, don't they? That was one of many questions that left me tremendously confused. My life was so unsettled. I wondered what the next step was in Nature's Plan.

My belief in human kindness – people as friends and companions – was gone. Despite the awful circumstances I was caught in, I'm certain. Everything happens for a reason.

I want a future. I want to look ahead, and move on to better, brighter days. I want to live – and love - but that will take someone being there for me. Right now, I'm alone – and I'm petrified with fear. Does anyone know I'm here?

Whatever anyone wishes may be, as everything stands now, I'm facing the end of my life. What are their criteria for rendering the ultimate judgment? Yesterday, I received a reprieve – a second chance at life. If only I can live, I'll use my time in the world to save others who deserve a better fate than what I've faced.

I'm trying to make sense of the conversation I hear between two of the people who work at the center where I'm being held.

"Remember the frisky beagle?" Cody responded clearing his throat.

DANIEL THE MIRACLE BEAGLE

"Yes, he was kind of cute. Why did they gas him, anyway? Andy asked.

"I don't know—I guess they thought no one wanted to adopt him."

"But did anyone try to find him a home?"

"Don't know—I just do what I'm told. It's a job," Cody blurted. He seemed a bit upset. "Also the rule here is that after four days, if a dog is not adopted, he's gassed!"

"Four days—that's absurd! Too bad. I bet lots of kids would have loved to have him as a pet."

"Did they really try to find him a home?" Cody asked.

"There is an ironic twist to this story. While he was in the gas chamber a man came looking to adopt a beagle."

I couldn't believe my ears. Someone came in to adopt me? The pain – and inequity – of losing millions of my precious animal friends to a system that snuffs out their lives is rooted in some people being "too busy". This has to stop. Life is a gift that is there to be shared.

"Well, the beagle is here and wagging his tail. He's the dog who just barked."

"Are you kidding me? How can that be? Didn't you put him in the gas chamber with the other dogs?" Andy exclaimed. I could see he was visibly fidgety and caught off guard.

"Yes he was in there. Just didn't go. Do you think we should try again?"

Oh no! : My mind began to reel. Don't send me back there again. Cody said that wouldn't happen. Was he having second thoughts? My heart was racing. I couldn't breathe. I want to live.

Please, please – don't end my time now! I'm asking for another miracle. I'll show everyone – everywhere – how special life is.

"We'll call him Daniel, after the biblical figure appointed prince by King Darius," Andy announced. "You remember the story - don't you, Cody? When the King's degree prohibiting prayer or the petitioning of any god or man except for the king was violated by Daniel, he was cast into the den of hungry lions, only to be delivered from all harm."

"That's a very appropriate name."

How thrilling to be named after a great biblical man. Now I have to live up to it and do great things. Will I be helped, as Daniel was?

"So what are you going to do with Daniel, Cody? Put him back in the gas chamber?"

"No, that's it. I'm letting him be. With all those fumes he inhaled he will probably lose it during the night. And if he doesn't, that means he should live. It had to be some kind of miracle. I've never seen any dog walk out like this beagle did. It was incredible. You had to see it with your own eyes to believe it. They were all wiped out inside. "

My prayer was answered. Infinite thanks. I promise I will be a good dog.

Now it would be up to loving people. Of course, I had to believe. Who else could I possibly trust?

"So - what do we have here?" a sweet, smiling woman asked. Her name was Karen, and she had appeared from nowhere.

"He's a beagle. Well - I guess we should say he's *the* beagle. Daniel walked out of the gas chamber - apparently unharmed." - Cody responded, actually looking proud.

"I'd like to take him to our shelter in Tennessee, and perhaps get him a nice family." - Karen replied. "He looks like a friendly, lovable pup."

I think I like this lady and her husband Michael. He patted me on the head and said some nice things about me. My tail was wagging at lightning speed. I was tingling with elation. Life can bring sweet answers to the greatest mysteries. There was no rhyme or reason to it all, but I felt elated. It wasn't really important to have all the answers to life's mysteries just yet.

Soon after, I was collared and transported to a different pound. I think I heard Karen and Michael mention a place called Schnauzer Savers Rescue of West Tennessee. I was still pretty much in a daze. Karen kept tickling me under the chin and asking me how I was feeling. Here were people filled with love and attention. Such a fine feeling to be given a real chance. Happy days were just beginning.

I lived with Karen and Michael's six beautiful schnauzers for the next several weeks.

"He's darling." Karen cooed, giving me a peck on the head. "Daniel has the most amazing will to live of any dog I have ever rescued, and it's just amazing. He just refuses to give up! Incredible."

"I can't believe they tried to gas such a beautiful, energetic pup," Michael added - flashing me a bright smile.

"Thankfully, our efforts with the Alabama Legislature and the other groups we addressed paid off," I heard Karen say. "As of next summer the gas chamber will be outlawed, and as of the end of next year it has to be dismantled and discarded."

What great news! Other innocent dogs in Alabama will not have to be victims of such a savage practice. I love Karen and Michael. If only everyone would be so passionate about defending the rights of innocent animals, we could all live together in blissful serenity.

Karen and Michael took me to the Veterinary Clinic for a complete physical.

"Good." The vet was very pleased. "No wax or inflammation. Everything looks good to me."

The checkup was nothing compared to what we'd all been through in the chamber. I can do this.

My blood tests were also amazing. "I think Daniel's a lucky dog to have spent over 20 minutes inhaling the deadliest poison fumes imaginable. It's unbelievable - I don't see any ill after-effects.", the Doc said.

The following day, after all the blood results were in, I was given a clean bill of health. My neutering came next – to help control the pet population.

"Since Eleventh Hour Rescue in New Jersey has agreed to take Daniel, I'm going to contact the transport coordinator for an Animal Rescue Flight Service.", Karen said.

Wow! Someone wants me! How cool is that? The Service is a non-profit group, whose pilots cover all costs for every element of flying abandoned dogs to rescue facilities for adoption. A pilot volunteered to fly me - and eleven other pups - to our new destinations. I eagerly awaited his arrival. He came around sunrise, and was totally on our side. I felt secure – and free.

The pilot was a great guy. He bent over, scooped me up and carried me to the airfield. About fifteen minutes after we got there, we were escorted into carriers and loaded on a small airplane.

We stopped at Greenville, NC and Easton, Maryland. We were very well cared for throughout the flight. After the plane took off from Easton, I wondered where I'd be going.

I found out when we landed in Caldwell, NJ. The pilot told me that this was my stop, and let me know that he would take me home, but that his two dogs were the limit where he lived. He gave me one of life's greatest gifts – a second chance.

At Caldwell's Fairfield Airport, I greeted my unexpected welcoming committee with a wagging tail. I had survived – and now I have a Fan Club! I was a celebrity! There were TV and newspaper reporters, along with an enthusiastic crowd. Here was Heaven on Earth. Linda Schiller, Jill and her family – people and pups – were precious friends, sharing freedom, respect, and great meals as my new life began.

My gratitude is infinite. I turn to Nature, and await its design for my life. I feel ready to meet my new family, believing that they will be exceptional in their love and clarity. It's in the stars.

There are 80 million pet dogs
in the United States.

CHAPTER 4
CROSSING THE THRESHOLD
THE " MEET AND GREET "
DANIEL'S TALE

Chapter Four

Crossing the Threshold: The "Meet and Greet"
Daniel's Tale

"**D**aniel, this is your big day," Jill said, stroking my head. My big day? I wondered what she meant. Would I be meeting new rescue dog friends here, or finding a new home – with a Forever Family?

Jill said that she was calling a man named Joe. I hadn't crossed paths with anyone by that name. Jill trusted and respected him, and a very lively conversation between them was underway as soon as the call got started.

Joe made a point of mentioning that he had heard all about the story of my miraculous survival – from many different sources. The discussion moved on to Jill's friend, Linda, and the huge, dramatic impact that Linda's relating the story of my salvation to an Awards Benefit had on the audience there. Linda said that silence filled the room, and no one had dared to take a breath as she described the swirl of events that had come my way.

I had a struck a very deep chord with Joe. He had called Linda again – several days later – and asked about my progress. Linda said that I was doing wonderfully, and that there were many offers – some with substantial donations included – from people who wanted to give me a Lifetime Home. There was even one potential adopter who had experienced a last minute change of heart about taking me in. Linda made it abundantly clear that I was a celebrity in the making, and that I needed to be part of a warm, affectionate family – one who could blend my being very widely known into a life of dignity and peace.

Joe mentioned that he had four dogs at home – Shelby, Spartacus, Rommel and Greta – and that I would greatly enjoy the pleasure of their gregarious company. When Linda replied that Joe should adopt me, he suggested a "meet and greet" – a chance for me to spend some time with Joe, his family, and their canine quartet. We'd all have a chance to see if the chemistry was there for me to live with them for the rest of my life.

The call between Jill and Joe confirmed that Jill would bring me over to Joe's home. They were on the same wavelength – there must be love all around. Joe had mentioned that he was a certified dog trainer. Good – that meant he would have all of our best interests at heart. What a tremendous joy to be loved by people who truly honored life. It would mean so much to take the next steps of my journey – and to send a message of all the lives that could be saved and made better – with people who truly understood why we were all here. Meeting four new friends to play with was more than I had ever dreamed of.

I was at my very best as Jill and I headed out for the "meet and greet". As we made our way in the car, I believed that everything would work out for the best. There had been a huge snowstorm the night before. Joe assured Jill that all was well at his home, and that everyone was filled with joy and anticipation for our time together. Joe came to greet us as we reached his house. There was an instant bond between us.

The initial round of hugs and kisses with Joe was soon followed by the first big test. With too much snow in the yard, we would all take a stroll around the block before heading inside. Joe and his wife, Geralynn, came around with Shelby and Spartacus. I walked right up to Shelby, and – within a minute – we were dancing together on our hind legs. We totally hit it off. When we went inside, Rommel and Greta greeted me as a brother. More love at first sight. The last question now had to be answered. How would Spartacus feel about me? Did he remember that this day was the 5th anniversary of his joining Joe's family as a rescue dog?

His emphatic response came very soon. He began to growl – slowly and softly at first – and then he let loose a bark. So far as he was concerned, this was his territory, and I was an intruder. His tail was still – and straight up. I responded by yelping, and our "conversation" carried on for several minutes. Joe stepped in, suggesting that we try another meeting the following week – to allow space and time for Spartacus to adjust to the idea of me as the newest member of the family.

And so, Jill and I headed back to her house. I was so excited that the first meeting went well enough for us to have another visit. Joe, Geralynn - and all the dogs, except Spartacus – had taken me into their hearts and home. I wanted – with all of my being – to be part of their amazing family. Joe would have to do everything – and more – to bring Spartacus around.

The days flew by to the following week. We were lucky to have a more pleasant day – and the run of Joe's yard – for our return visit. I greeted Joe, then headed straight for Shelby. We picked up right where we'd left off. With Greta and Rommel totally in tune, Spartacus had to make his feelings known. He came out with a "Remember – I'm the boss." bark, which was perfectly fine with me. It meant so much for me to live here that he could feel free to make his statement, and I'd be glad to let him keep his territory. Joe and Jill agreed that the ice had been broken between Spartacus and me. Joe wanted to adopt me!

Everything I had wished for and dreamed about – that had kept me alive – was coming true. I was overwhelmed with joy. Parents! Sisters and brothers! I twirled around in circles. I'd never known such love.

A few days later, after the final details had been set, Jill's husband, Mark, brought me back to Joe's house – this time for me to join the family. Hugs and kisses shared with Joe and Geralynn, the next love fest with Shelby, and then – as we settled on the pillow together – a great first night's sleep in my new home, with my dear brother – Spartacus.

There are over 250 million pets
of every variety in the United States.

Nearly 9,000 species call the Gálapagos Islands and their surrounding waters home.

The Gálapagos Islands are a
UNESCO World Heritage Site.

There are 9 million known species on Earth.

6.5 million of Earth's species
were found on land.

2.2 million of Earth's species dwell
in ocean depths.

Scientists estimate that 86% of all species on land are yet to be catalogued.

Scientists estimate that 91% of all species in the seas are yet to be catalogued.

CHAPTER 5
ANDERSON COOPER
JOE AND DANIEL VISIT " ANDERSON "

Chapter Five

Anderson Cooper
Joe & Daniel Visit "Anderson"

T he swirl of events around Joe and Daniel began to gain momentum at a dizzying speed.

A huge rally near Philadelphia - soon after Daniel joined Joe and Joe's family - was vital in working toward the passage of Daniel's Law, a tribute to Daniel's miraculous survival through a bill to keep all shelter pets alive until they are rescued, that began its rapid ascent through the State Legislature in Pennsylvania.

A Media explosion followed. Coverage poured out - on broadcast and cable television stations in the New York, New Jersey and Philadelphia markets, over Social Media, on the Internet, and in several major New York Metro Area newspapers.

An evocative story in The New York Post was followed with a breakthrough article - filled with photographs and details of Daniel's new life in a loving home - that appeared in The Newark Star Ledger.

The New York Daily News ran a compelling extract of the Star Ledger's coverage, and the road to National Media was next to open.

Network Radio interviews - with WCBS /NEWSRADIO 880 in New York, the Flagship Station of the CBS Radio Network, and on NPR/National Public Radio - soon followed, reaching millions with Daniel's compelling message in minutes.

Anderson Cooper was next to express an interest. Mr. Cooper - currently the anchor of "Anderson Cooper 360" and CNN's continuous political coverage, has co-anchored "AMERICAN MORNING " and " NEWSNIGHT " and co-hosted specials - "Planet In Peril" and "All Star Heroes " - on CNN, is a correspondent for CBS NEWS "60 MINUTES", and hosts "Anderson" - a nationally syndicated talk show.

He is one of the most highly accomplished and respected journalists in contemporary broadcast and cable television. He has travelled to many colorful and intriguing corners of the world in the course of his reporting. His time at ABC included co-anchoring ABC WORLD NEWS NOW and hosting the first two seasons of THE MOLE - a reality game show. Mr. Cooper started his television career at the educational Channel One, where he beamed broadcasts of students fighting for their freedom in Burma to middle school and high school classrooms throughout the United States.

Anderson has also established his credentials in the cultural realm. His memoir, "Dispatches From The Edge " - describing his reporting experiences in Sri Lanka, Africa, Iraq and Louisiana - topped the New York Times Bestseller List. His freelance writing has led to articles in "Details" and numerous other magazines. The son of American fashion and social icon Gloria Vanderbilt, he is the voice of The Narrator for the Broadway revival of "How To Succeed In Business Without Really Trying".

The phone call from the Associate Producer of "Anderson" sent Joe, Daniel and the whole family into a whirlwind of excitement. A limousine would arrive at the house the next day to take Joe, Daniel and Geralynn to the taping of the show.

The chemistry ignited between Daniel and Anderson as soon as Mr. Cooper arrived for a pre-taping visit in the Green Room at the studio where "Anderson" is produced. Daniel jumped over to Anderson and smothered him with love. Anderson showed himself to be a devoted lover of animals, getting down on his knees to romp with his new, special friend.

The love fest continued when it was time for Daniel to meet Anderson and the audience for the taping. Daniel's enthusiastic showering of Anderson with love as they met before the lights and cameras led Mr. Cooper to say: "Daniel, I wish all my guests would do that."

As Daniel prowled around - and under - the furniture on the set, Anderson was a lively and gracious host. Joe and Geralynn related the full story of Daniel's miracle. The message was enhanced when the show turned to comments from the audience, and Linda - who had been so instrumental in Daniel's rescue and adoption - delivered a poignant plea to bring families and pets who want to share their lives together.

Rounds of enthusiastic applause rang out to celebrate Daniel's appearance on "Anderson".

Daniel's warm and courageous message of life and beauty had come shining through.

The fabulous experience with "Anderson" would soon open another amazing door for Daniel and his new family on television - to be viewed half-way around the world.

Cats were considered to be sacred
in Ancient Egypt.

CHAPTER 6
ASHAI TV / JAPAN
WINDOW TO THE ORIENT

Chapter Six

Ashai TV/Japan
Window to the Orient

As Daniel's story began to reach further and further into the Media environment, the world soon started to take notice - and respond.

On the heels of the triumphant "Anderson" appearance, a call came in to Joe from a producer at the New York offices of Ashai TV/Japan - one of that nation's largest and most prestigious networks.

Affiliated with Ashai Shimbun - Japan's greatest, most widely respected newspaper, equivalent to The New York Times in the United States - Ashai TV was established in the late 1950's as a for-profit educational network. Such a status was - and remains - extremely unique in the world of television.

Daniel's story was particularly compelling to the people of Japan. Many animals there - as in the U.S. - needed to be rescued and adopted, and the northern part of the country had been over-whelmed by a combined natural and societal disaster, which had made the situation there - for people and their fellow creatures alike - even more profound.

Within days of the call from Ashai in New York, a 3 person team - producer, reporter and cameraman - arrived to film Daniel, Joe, and the rest of the family.

The respect and affection that flowed from the Ashai TV crew in the several hours they shared at Joe's house were an expression of both an extraordinary culture and universal human values. Daniel was a shining star over the course of the production. His romping, connecting to the dogs and people all around him and infinite zest for life made for marvelous television. The Ashai crew had come bearing gifts - toys for Daniel that he relished from the second he received them. The greatest gift - for everyone - was the comity and deep unity of purpose that become a vital element for all who had come together to create the video for an audience half-way around the world.

The report that resulted was such a sensation that Ashai TV expanded its commitment to broadcasting Daniel's story - initially to be shown as a 1-minute nugget on a single night. Instead, the network went all-out to fully raise Public Awareness with a 5 minute + Daniel feature, including introductions addressing the overall situation of animal rights and rescue and an excellent development of context - on 3 consecutive nights - nationwide throughout Japan.

Having gained a global platform, Daniel's mission was well under-way.

Reaching the largest audience, as swiftly as possible, to do the most good for people and pets would fill every day with love and determination.

Politics, and passing laws, were vital to the process of creating a life-supporting environment - in the U.S. and far beyond.

Daniel's Law was a key element in providing solutions.

Domestic dogs originated
with the Eurasian Grey Wolf.

The present lineage of domestic dogs
arose over 15,000 years ago.

Links to wolves, foxes and dogs date back nearly 60 million years.

The genetic lineage of domesticated cats dates back 100,000 years.

The Near Eastern Wildcat still roams
the deserts of the region,
and has been an Animal Companion
to people for over 12,000 years.

The Amazon rain forest has the highest biodiversity of any habitat.

The Koala's lineage dates back
40 million years.

The Blue Whale's sound - at 188 decibels - is
loudest in the Animal Kingdom,
and can be detected over 800 kilometres
(500 miles) away.

CHAPTER 7

SEN. DINNIMAN AND SETON HALL
DANIEL'S LAW

Chapter Seven

Sen. Dinniman and Seton Hall
Daniel's Law

Daniel's impact on the political scene started with a huge rally - just outside of Philadelphia - soon after he joined Joe and Joe's family.

Pennsylvania was on its way to becoming the 20th state to pass legislation that would protect the lives of all so-called "shelter" animals until they are able to be rescued, adopted, and brought to loving homes and families.

The movement to advance the cause of animal rights and welfare has evolved on two fronts - success on a state-by-state basis, and with the development of organizations who are coordinating nationally toward the goal of passing federal legislation. As more and more states pass meaningful legislation, the environment for action in Washington will be increasingly dynamic.

Daniel immediately established a deep, warm bond at the rally with Pennsylvania State Senator Andy Dinniman, a very socially conscious legislator with extensive experience in state and local government. Sen. Dinniman introduced Daniel to the enthusiastic crowd, which responded with a chorus of cheers and applause.

Daniel's Law - named for Daniel as a tribute to his miraculous survival - is vitally important, because Daniel's story serves as a focal point for millions of people to more fully and rapidly identify with the infinitely valuable role that our animal companions play in improving the quality of our lives as they share their love with us.

The rapid progress of Daniel's Law as it advanced through the Pennsylvania State Senate serves as a model for future victories throughout the nation. Within weeks of its introduction in Committee, Daniel's law was speeding its way to consideration by the full Senate. If all goes well, Pennsylvania - the Keystone State - will soon join the list of states that have expressed their awareness of a more beautiful and humane alternative for animals and people.

With the news of Daniel's tremendous influence on the Pennsylvania State Senate swiftly reaching a national audience, Seton Hall University School of Law extended an invitation for Daniel to visit with professors and students for a discussion of the legal, moral, ethical and humane elements of animal rights legislation.

Seton Hall Law School - founded in 1951 - is the only private Law School in New Jersey, and is the top-ranked of the three law schools in the state.

Professor Robert Martin - who had previously served in the New Jersey State Legislature for 15 years - was host to Daniel and Joe. After introducing Daniel to the vibrant assembly, Professor Martin asked Joe to tell the story of Daniel's miracle.

Seton Hall's Student Animal Legal Defense Fund has structured initiatives for the rights of companion animals, animals in entertainment, those bred for experimental use, and wildlife.

Harvard, Stanford, Georgetown, Duke and UCLA are among the prominent universities offering courses in Animal Law. Today, over 120 Law Schools - including every leading school in the nation - offer courses in this vital field of law to future attorneys, all of whom are dedicated to applying the legal system to defending and maintaining the rights of animals to live with care and dignity. The reputations - and geographic distribution - of such programs provide the perfect foundation for state and federal laws to be passed and put into action.

The group at Seton Hall agreed with Professor Martin that the highest goal for Daniel was advocacy on a national scale. Professor Martin observed that a single incident - such as Daniel's miracle - can spark a movement and turn a cause into law.

Movements to enact Daniel's Law are beginning to catch fire in Michigan, Texas and Massachusetts, with coordination on a state-by-state basis - toward enacting Federal legislation - to follow.

Daniel's phenomenal influence in the political process expresses the power of a single loving, innocent puppy to generate the momentum for widespread, positive change, greater understanding of the value of bonding with animals, and higher Quality Of Life.

Hummingbirds possess such agility and skill that they can fly backwards.

CHAPTER 8

BEAGLES AND THE WORLD
FOREVER FRIENDS

Chapter Eight

Beagles and the World

Forever Friends

Daniel carries on the proud history of the deep, phenomenal bond that exists between beagles and their human companions.

The Beagle is a member of the Hound Group, and is known as a scent hound for their great sense of smell and tracking instinct. Beagles are valuable in detecting prohibited agricultural imports and food around the world, and are prized as pets for their intelligence, sunny disposition, moderate size and genetic strength.

Beagle-type dogs have existed for over 2000 years. The origins of contemporary Beagles trace back to Ancient Greece, around the 5th century BC. Xenophon - in his "Treatise on Hunting" ("Cynegeticus") - takes note of a Beagle-like hound who sensed hares by scent and followed them on foot.

The Forest Laws of Canute - who ruled over England, Denmark, Norway and parts of Sweden shortly after 1000 BC - appear to confirm that breeds similar to the beagle were present in England before 1016. In the 11th century, William the Conqueror brought the Talbot Hound - derived from the St. Hubert hound, developed in the 8th century - to Britain. English Talbots were crossed with greyhounds for extra speed, and - though long extinct - probably gave rise to the Southern Hound, an ancestor of the modern-day Beagle.

From medieval times, the term "Beagle" was used as a description for smaller hounds who, differed considerably from the contemporary breed. Miniature breeds of Beagle-type dogs were known from the times of Edward II and Henry VII, who both had packs of Glove Beagles - so named since they were small enough to fit on a glove.

Queen Elizabeth I kept a breed known as the Pocket Beagle, which stood 8 to 9 inches at the shoulder and was small enough to fit in a "pocket" or saddlebag. Elizabeth I referred to the dogs as her "singing Beagles," and often allowed her Pocket Beagles to cavort with guests at her Royal Table as part of entertainment at meals and celebrations.

19th century sources refer to the Glove and Pocket Beagle breeds interchangeably. The early 17th century writer and poet Gervase Markham described a beagle small enough to sit on a man's hand, and to the "little small mitten beagle, which may be companion for a ladies kirtle, and in the field will run as cunningly as any hound whatere, only their musick is very small like reeds."

Standards for the pocket Beagle were drawn up so late as 1901, and - though genetic lines are now extinct - modern breeders have attempted to rescue the variety.

The 18th century saw the development of two breeds in Britain - the Southern Hound and the North Country Beagle, or Northern Hound. These Beagle-like lines came close to extinction as they were bred with larger breeds - such as the Stag Hound - but farmers ensured their survival by maintaining packs to protect against rabbits.

The basis for the modern Beagle breed arose in the 1830's, with the establishment of a pack by Reverend Phillip Honeywood of Essex. Honeywood's small Beagles stood about 10 inches at the shoulder and were pure white, with bloodlines from Harriers, North Country Beagles and Southern Hounds. Prince Albert and Lord Winterton also had Beagle packs at the time - and Royal Favour led to renewed interest in the breed - but Honeywell's pack was regarded as the finest of the three.

Two strains - the rough and smooth-coated varieties - evolved from Honeywell's devotion. The rough-coated Beagle survived to the early 20th century - with records of one even appearing at a dog show so late as 1969 - but the variety is now extinct, having probably been absorbed into the standard Beagle bloodline.

In the 1840's, a standard Beagle bloodline began to develop. The distinction between the North Country Beagle and Southern hound had dissolved, though a significant variation in size, character and behavior remained.

In 1856, " The Manual of British Rural Sports " divided Beagles into 4 varieties - Medium/Dwarf (Lapdog)/Fox, and rough-coated (terrier).

By 1887, any threat of extinction to the Beagle in England had waned.

The Beagle Club was formed in 1890, and the first standard was drawn up at the same time. The Association of Masters of Harriers and Beagles was formed in 1891. Both organizations aimed to further the best interests of the breed, and were keen to produce a standard Beagle type.

Beagles entered the United States around the 1840's. The first dogs varied in quality. In the early 1870's, General Richard Rowett started serious attempts at quality bloodlines when he imported Beagles from England to Illinois. His Beagles formed the basis for the first American standard, which he drew up - with consultations - in 1887.

The Beagle was accepted as a breed by the American Kennel Club (AKC) in 1884, and his companionship with Forever Families enjoyed a rapid spread worldwide throughout the 20th century.

Beagle Shows in the United Kingdom were wildly popular. A regular show at Petersborough - started in 1889 - was taken over by the Association of Masters of Harriers and Beagles when that organization was formed, two years later.

The Beagle Club in the UK held their first show in 1896. Regular showings led to a uniform Beagle type, and only the outbreak of World War I - when all shows were suspended - interrupted the Beagle's phenomenal success and popularity. The period between the wars led to a renewed struggle for the Beagle's survival in Britain, and included the end of the Pocket Beagle. Interest in Beagles greatly revived after World War II.

North America has shown tremendous hospitality to Beagles. The National Beagle Club of America was formed in 1888, and - by 1901- a Beagle had a won a Best In Show Title. The world-renowned Westminster Kennel Show awarded a number of prizes to Beagles in 1928, and in 1939 show Beagle Champion Meadowlark Draughtsman was named top-winning American-bred Dog Of The Year. In 2008, K-Run's Park Me In First (Uno) was the first Beagle ever to capture the most highly coveted Best In Show at Westminster.

As Daniel explodes into Media, Politics, and Popular Culture, he heads toward joining Snoopy - hero and star of the iconic PEANUTS comics by Charles Schultz - in the pantheon of World's Most Beloved Beagles. Snoopy - who sleeps on the roof of his red doghouse, which is filled with Fine Art, designer furniture and lighting, great accoutrements and a "rec room" - is a child of the Universe, and friend to all, who is blessed with infinite insight and sensitivity. As PEANUTS has leapt from the comics pages of newspapers all over the world to adaptations for stage, screen, and television, Snoopy's role as Beagle

Ambassador - and his influence in fostering love and understanding between people and Beagles - has grown exponentially.

Beagles are celebrated in the works of such immortals as Shakespeare, John Dryden, Henry Fielding and Alexander Pope's translation of Homer's "Illiad." Walt Disney has featured Beagles in a number of films ("Beagle Boys" / "Beegle Beagle"), and they have appeared in such other films as "Cats And Dogs" (and its sequel), "Audition," and "The Royal Tenenbaums". Beagles have appeared on television in such series as "Star Trek: Enterprise," "The Wonder Years," and the BBC perennial "EastEnders."

Charles Darwin's voyage on HMS Beagle - the ship was named for the breed - was much of the inspiration for his "On the Origin of Species," and Britain's Planetary Exploration Programme went on to name a Mars Lander Beagle 2 - to honor both Darwin and our ongoing bond with Beagle companions everywhere.

Daniel's joining such exalted company, and his entering the stream of such remarkable history, is an inspiration - to him and to everyone around the world who is committed to raising the level of awareness, and resulting success, in serving as champions for the cause of Animal Rights and Welfare.

There are 20,000 known species of bees.

CHAPTER 9

VISION
DANIEL'S MISSION

Chapter Nine

Vision
Daniel's Mission

Daniel's miracle story - and his mission - are poised to make a difference around the world.

In the United States, federal legislation saving wonderful "shelter" pets - uniting worthy animal companions with people who are ready, willing and able to give them a lifetime of love and dignity - will be developed in tandem with progress in every state that is yet to pass similar, humane bills into law.

Contact between legislators in states that have successfully established such laws and everyone - legislators and committed groups - in states where laws must be enacted will greatly hasten the momentum of positive, permanent change, leading to a quantum leap on the national level.

Daniel's Law - and Daniel - will stand at the forefront of greater Public Awareness, motivation to succeed, and very rewarding results.

A society is seen - with great justification - as fulfilling its values when there is meaningful help, encouragement and understanding flowing to those who most have to be protected and spoken for - whose needs are the greatest.

Daniel's message of courage, strength and love is an inspiration to people and organizations - in America and beyond - who are dedicated to the cause of Animal Rights and Rescue.

In coming months and years, Daniel and Joe will be reaching out to - and accomplishing their mission with - such remarkable advocates for loving animal friends as:

Adopt A Pet / Adopt A Beagle - Funded By Purina / Beagle Rescue / Rational Animal – NYC / AKC - American Kennel Club Breed

Rescue / SOS (Save Our Snoopies) Beagle / Beagle Rescue Foundation Of America / The Eleventh Hour / The Last Post / National Animal Rescue And Sheltering Coalition / The Humane Society Of The United States / National Animal Welfare Society / Born Free USA - The Animal Protection Institute (API) / Wheels Of Hope - The Mayor's Alliance For New York's Animals / IFAW-International Fund For Animal Welfare / International Animal Rescue / CWOB - Compassion Without Borders, International Dog Rescue / Northwest International Pet Rescue / WSPA -World Society For The Protection Of Animals / Animalia International / FAO - Food And Agricultural Organisation Of The United Nations, and many more.

Internationally, programs are in the process of coordination toward the passage of a United Nations Universal Declaration Of Animal Welfare (UDAW) , which would vastly accelerate progress on a global scale.

Daniel's celebrity in Japan - emanating from his national appearance on Ashai Television - is the foundation toward collaboration with:

Search Dog Foundation (SDF) / Humane Society International / World Vets / Japan Cat Network / Animal Garden, Nigata / Animal Friends, Nigata / Heart – Tokushima / Animal Refuge, Kansai / Japan's Cat Island / The Animal Miracle Network Foundation / Global Animal Foundation / Tokyo ARK / Osaka ARK, and others.

Animal Sanctuaries provide love and peace for pets on a permanent basis, while educating the public, around the world.

Around the globe, Daniel and Joe will promote such loving places as:

Warrawong and Edgar's Mission (Australia) / Parque Machia, Parque Ambue Ari, and Parque Jacj Cuisi (Bolivia) / Aspen Valley, Big Sky Ranch, and Constance Creek (Canada) / Project Tiger, Corbett National Park, Govind Pashu Vihar, Great Himilayan National Park, and Singalila National Park (India) / Satya Sai and Dogs Aid (Ireland) / Hingol National Park and Rann Of Kutch (Pakistan) / Elephant Nature Park (Thailand) / Zwa Rhino (Uganda) / and - in the United Kingdom - Assisi, Ferne, Hartland Wildlife Rescue, Hillside, Qolas, Springflower, Thornberry, and Willows.

With the mosaic of rights, rescue, and preservation that exists throughout the planet, many other centers and refuges will be integrated as Daniel's Global Campaign evolves.

In the United States, Daniel and Joe will spread the word of the great work by The American Sanctuary Association and such healing centers as :

Friends For Life and Healing Hearts (Arizona) / Harvest Home and Living Free (California) / Wild Animal and Peaceful Prairie (Colorado) / Jungle Friends Primate and Big Cat Rescue (Florida) / Poplar Spring (Maryland) / Maple Farm (Massachusetts) / Graceful Acres (Michigan) / St. Francis (Mississippi) / Large Animal Rescue and Rolling Dog Ranch (Montana) / Animal Ark Wildlife and Safe Haven Rescue Zoo (Nevada) / For The Animals and Under My Wing (New Jersey) / Heart And Soul and Safe Haven (New Mexico) / Oasis, Woodstock Farm and Catskills (New York) / Carolina Raptor and Faithful Friends (North Carolina) / Happy Trails and Noah's Ark (Ohio) / Safari Interactive and Free To Live (Oklahoma) / Chimps, Inc. and Sanctuary One (Oregon) / Norman Bird (Rhode Island) / Elephant - and Tiger Haven (Tennessee) / Bat World, Thunder Paws, Whiskerville, Welcome Home Barnyard and Cleveland Amory Black Beauty Ranch (Texas) / Best Friends (Utah) , and Home For Life (Washington) in furthering understanding and development of these havens.

Daniel's presence in today's Media Universe - already established on Television (Ashai TV / Japan and Anderson Cooper's "Anderson"), Network Radio (WCBS / Newsradio 880 - New York and NPR / National Public Radio), Magazines (" Purina Animal Rescue " / " Cesar Millan - Dog Whisperer " and " THE WEEK ") , Internet (danielthe-beagle.com / linked to flowerpowercreative.com), and with a rapidly growing number of followers on Social Media - is ready to explode in the very near future.

Collaboration with the widest possible range of Media Outlets, dedicated groups, and individuals of courage and determination will link Daniel to millions of people - with caring hearts and open minds - all over the world.

Daniel's miracle will lead to an infinity of happy endings - for pets and people.

Daniel is the living, loving, dancing, beautiful, vibrant proof that sharing a miracle is one of life's greatest gifts.

Lions are the only cats who live in groups, known as prides.

ABOUT THE AUTHOR

JOE DWYER

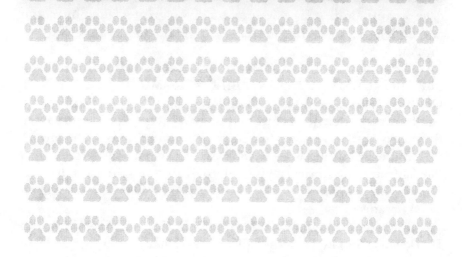

ABOUT THE AUTHOR / JOE DWYER

Joe Dwyer's mission with Daniel - The Miracle Beagle - is the latest chapter in a life dedicated to sharing, caring, healing, the greater good of humankind, and infinite love for our Animal Friends and Companions.

" DANIEL " is Joe's fourth book.

His previous works are :

" SHELBY'S GRACE " - The story of Joe's rescue of Shelby, an abandoned pit bull pup who - with Joe's love and care - is now a certified Therapy Dog. Joe and Shelby's current journeys serve people with physical and emotional challenges. As another element of their outreach, Joe's speaking appearances with Shelby - at schools and civic organizations - place lively emphasis on greater communication and understanding as the answer to bullying in modern society.

And :

" THE DOG ATE MY HOMEWORK - OR DID HE ? : THE COMPLETE GUIDE TO ACCOUNTABILITY FROM THE DOG'S POINT OF VIEW " - Joe's kaleidoscopic exploration of the remarkable range - and variety - of elements involved in establishing the finest foundation - Goal Setting / Integrity / Honest Communication / Teamwork / Harmony / Enthusiasm - for Success in personal and professional life. Through the stories of his family of dogs, Joe's theme is that our Canine Companions can show us the way to fulfilling our most cherished dreams.

Joe also contributed to " ROADMAP TO SUCCESS " - Along with Dr. Deepak Chopra, Dr. Ken Blanchard and many other experts in an astonishing number of fields, Joe was interviewed on the topic of actualizing the right direction for successful Business Strategies. Joe discussed The Dog's View Of Success with David Wright - President of ISN Works and Insight Publishing.

Joe's background also embraces experience as a Motivational Speaker / Corporate and Civic Mediator / Certified Life Coach / Certified Dog Trainer and Board Member of numerous Animal Rights And Rescue Groups.

Joe's interest in Martial Arts - and the Orient - has evolved to his becoming a Third Degree Black Belt in GoJu Ryu Karate.

Joe earned a degree in chemistry from Rutgers University's Newark College Of Arts And Sciences.

Joe - with his wife, Geralynn, daughter Jenna and son Joe - calls Nutley, New Jersey home.

Tigers are the largest of the Big Cats,
and have continued to evolve
for over 2 million years.

ABOUT FLOWER POWER CREATIVE

ABOUT FLOWER POWER CREATIVE

FLOWER POWER CREATIVE is a Multi-Media /Multi-Platform, solution - oriented Organisation and website - www.flowerpower creative.com - structured, in a universe of creativity and concepts, to provide people around the world with the energy and focus to power the momentum of solutions.

FLOWERPOWERCREATIVE.com's 5 Platforms - POLITICS / MUSIC AND FINE ARTS / WOMEN'S RIGHTS / ENVIRON-MENT / TECHNIQUES - address topics that are vital in their immediacy and timeless in their essence.

DANIEL'S MISSION, FPC's collaboration with Daniel - The Miracle Beagle - and Joe Dwyer, is the next phase in an ongoing series of Creative Concepts.

Flower Power Creative has announced the development of World Artists For Peace - a cultural and musical collaboration aimed at promoting positive change through the works of many of the world's most influential artists.

Inspired by The Beatles original concept for Apple, the record label intended as a creative outlet for the legendary rock band and others, World Artists for Peace will join with musicians, visual artists, writers, poets, and the widest variety of talent in the Fine Arts for a series of Projects and Events to support Peace Initiatives around the globe.

The Flower Power Creative / New York Celebrates George Harrison Concert - Starred music legend / back-to-back GRAMMY winner Roberta Flack and featured 6 other groups in a kaleidoscopic interpretation of the immortal Beatle / Traveling Wilbury / Solo

Artist's Music, Spirit and Vision. The Concert was held at the renowned New York Society For Ethical Culture, on Central Park West.

The Flower Power Creative - Beatles / 45 Shea Stadium Celebration - at Citi Field - was a night that recognised the largest live event in Music History at the time of its presentation - The Beatles first Concert at Shea Stadium in New York.

The Beatles performance - before an ecstatic crowd of over 56,000 - was the foundation for over 90,000 attending The Monterey Pop Festival, and over 500,000 at Woodstock.

An all-ladies tribute band performed the same set that The Beatles had played at Shea, and Sid Bernstein - the man who brought the Beatles to America, which propelled them to the world - was Guest Of Honour. Videos of the Concert at Shea added another phenomenal dimension to an electrifying Event.

Co-Founders Douglas Levison - CEO / CREATIVES - and Neil Chaimas - MUSIC EDITOR / CONCEPTUAL ADVISOR - derive their insight and inspiration from the massive wave of social change, along with the explosion of Creative Expressions, of the 1960's generally and The Beatles in particular.

DOUGLAS LEVISON'S background embraces Visual and Graphic Arts - NYU Film Programme / School Of Visual Arts, New York / DCTV - NYC / Academy Of Art University, San Francisco - including Film, Computer Graphics, Video, Photography, and Drawing. Mr. Levison also studied Political Science, History, Sociology, Cinema and Art at The University of California, Berkeley and Clark University, and Law at NYU.

NEIL CHAIMAS has pursued his passion for music in Workshops with Jazz legend Barry Harris, at The New York School of Commercial Music, and at Swing University / Jazz at Lincoln Centre, hosted by Jazz History icon Phil Schaap. Mr. Chaimas has written original compositions in a broad range of musical modalities.

Mr. Chaimas earned a BA in Psychology at Clark University, which included studies in Biochemistry, Genetics, and Creative Writing, followed by Postgraduate Research in Psychobiology at Clark that led to a breakthrough in the application of NGF (Nerve Growth Factor) - which allowed for behavioural recovery subsequent to brain damage.

The vision of Flower Power Creative is contributive to a world of greater Peace, harmony and understanding - based upon the actualisation of the fullest communication of Creative Concepts to people everywhere.

Owls live on every continent except
Antarctica, and have the best hearing
of all birds.

ACKNOWLEDGEMENTS

JOE DWYER

JOE DWYER / ACKNOWLEDGEMENTS

For all of the positive energy that led to Daniel's Miracle.

To my family - My wife, Geralynn, and my children - Jenna and Joe - for their infinite Love and support.

To my parents - For their guidance, and the wonderful example they set.

To our 4 loving pups - Rommel, Shelby, Greta and Spartacus - Daniel's devoted family and playmates, and a marvelous source of joy.

To my " brother, " Fritz - My constant Canine Companion, from childhood through my teenage years.

To Eleventh Hour Rescue - For their instrumental role in Daniel's journey to New Jersey, and into our home.

To Flower Power Creative - Doug Levison and Neil Chaimas, for their Creativity, Clarity, and Grace.

The Toucan's large, colourful bill
is 19 centimetres (7.5 inches) long.

ACKNOWLEDGEMENTS
FLOWER POWER CREATIVE

FLOWER POWER CREATIVE /
ACKNOWLEDGEMENTS

Flower Power Creative is most grateful for the magnificent support - in every element of evolution - resonating from :

Mr. George Regan, B.J. Finnell, the Boston Home Office, Nicole Glor and The New York Team of Regan Communications Group. Their belief in bringing a vision of Creativity and Solutions fully to life is an infinite inspiration.

Mr. Frank Silk, Velislava Atanasova, Caleb Kester and the phenomenal team at americaneagle.com. The beauty, stream of Consciousness, depth and vibrancy of flowerpowercreative.com are the result of our warm and dynamic collaboration.

Mr. Victor Ganzi. A beacon light of World Culture and Commerce, Mr. Ganzi's grace, insights and excellent orientation to the greater good are constant values to be treasured, and essential to realising dreams.

The American Bald Eagle's wingspan
ranges from 72 to 90 inches.

SPECIAL THANKS

SPECIAL THANKS -

To Sue Falduto, for the marvelous Outdoor Portraits of Daniel.

And

For the infinitely generous contribution of the
White Motif Portraits, by Anonymous Friends.